As I Cry Out To Heaven

As I Cry Out To Heaven

Elias Nemark Kasunga

Foreword by Pamela Austin

RESOURCE *Publications* • Eugene, Oregon

AS I CRY OUT TO HEAVEN

Resource Publications
An Imprint of Wipf and Stock Publishers
199 W. 8th Ave., Suite 3
Eugene, OR 97401

www.wipfandstock.com

PAPERBACK ISBN: 978-1-6667-3275-7
HARDCOVER ISBN: 978-1-6667-2679-4
EBOOK ISBN: 978-1-6667-2680-0

.   OCTOBER 18, 2021 2:35 PM

To God
My maker, my author of life,
the only one who can answer when I ask,
"*why am I really here?*"

To my Brothers and Sisters
Being imperfect is the first step,
to get you closer to the perfect God.

TABLE OF CONTENTS

Chapter 2
FOUND BY GRACE, EMBRACED BY LOVE

Chapter 3
BETWEEN VALLEYS AND HILLS

Chapter 4
A FORMER SINNER, A NEW DISCIPLE

Chapter 5
THE LOST PROVERBS

Chapter 6
A LETTER TO MY FUTURE WIFE

Chapter 7
AS I WALK INTO ETERNITY

FOREWORD

WHEN ELIAS FIRST MESSAGED me to ask if he could send me something, I had no idea what to expect. I was not aware that he was a Poet, so this book was a wonderful surprise.

I had intended to just glance at it but as soon as I started reading, I found myself completely immersed. I read it all in one sitting and then called Elias immediately. When he answered, I found myself speechless because there was so much I was still processing.

There is a beautiful rawness to Elias's writing. It digs deep into the heart because it tunnels into those secret places we tend to keep hidden and brings them to light.

One thing I have learned in life is that everyone tends to think they are a "*worse sinner*" than everyone else. We assume no one has battled the emotions and temptations we have battled. We keep our battles a secret so that no one knows our shame. But then someone like Elias comes forward and puts these experiences and emotions into words and people realize they are not the only one. This book reminds us that even though we may be on different battlefields, with different enemies, we all face spiritual battles.

I pray as you read this book that you allow your soul to embrace the highs and the lows that relate to your own personal journey. May the words encourage you and may they fill you with hope.

Pastor Pamela Austin

INTRODUCTION

Dear Reader,
as I cry out to heaven,
I present God with my sins and transgressions,
and in this bitter cry,
I give Him all my filthy addictions,
I'm not an orphan in this world,
I am a child asking for his Father's forgiveness,
His blood on the cross did that work,
and I have set to get my heart to accept it.

As you read these words of psalms,
I pray to relate to your weakness,
for there's no sin, no mistake, and no affliction
that can cast you away from His compassion,
and when you decide to cry out to heaven,
promise you'll remember that He listens,
for He can relate to all your flaws,
as He too was also tempted.

with love, *Elias Kasunga.*

CHAPTER 1

THE REPENTER

"Mirror mirror on the wall, who's the Worst Sinner of all?"

—THE WORST SINNER

I Made a Mistake

My reflection in the mirror is foreign,
my eyes haven't met each other in ages,
I haven't seen my face a while,
nor the smile that was once innocent,
my shame has covered my identity,
my addiction has become my name,
(*and my "also-known-as"*
is synonymous with my deepest regrets)
I made a mistake!
a repeated one, to God and humanity,
I made a mistake!
of which a death sentence is not enough,
a thousand deaths cannot atone,
I made a mistake!
a repeated one, to God and humanity.

The Worst Sinner: Part 1

He cried with tears of blood,
the *Worst Sinner* was nothing,
until his inner man took the turn in weeping,
his soul was hurt but his body rejoicing,
"*keep going now!*"
insisted his heart without thinking,
but how can he keep on going?
in denial, hypocrisy and acting?
while the conflict within him keeps creeping,
with every part of him constantly screaming,
"*choose me! choose me! choose me!*"
but what if instead, he chooses his maker?
who doesn't scream but He's still whispering,
"*you'll do better, if you only choose Me.*"

My Younger Days

I remember my younger days,
when my greatest sin was to lie to my mother
on the days I skipped school to play.

I remember my younger days,
when I went before a Priest and confessed my sins,
when I could narrate from the thought to
the very action of sin.

I remember my younger days,
when my mistakes did not carry regrets,
when my heart could live with the consequences,
when my mind could handle the punishment.

I remember my younger days,
when I could blame my age for my omissions,
when I could hide behind my environment,
when I thought maturity could change my ways,

those were the good old days.

The Worst Sinner: Part 2

Inside the cage he cannot stay,
the *Worst Sinner* is wearing away,
his soul can see his body decay,
for like a dog on a leash he's led astray,
he knows Jesus gives life, not yesterday but today,
(*but there's this sin that knocks on him,*
daily on a day to day)
he wishes his way through life,
with a bit of prayer kept at bay,
and he knows he's not a "*Daniel*",
twenty-one days with no play?
but this truth he keeps at heart,
"*no prayer, no gain.*"

Alarmed

You sound an alarm
loud enough for me to hear,
The sound of Your warning
is heard deep inside my heart,
I hear Your voice say to me,
"*leave this life of sin,*
it's not too late to run back to me"
You call out my name
as I walk shamelessly in my transgressions,
But not even my past could stop you from saying,
"*my child, my child,*
come to me and you'll be free."

Tired

I'm tired of cutting down the fruits of sin,
while leaving its roots deep under,
I'm tired of hoping for a change tomorrow,
only to go deeper into my sorrow,
I'm tired of repenting twice and thrice,
for me to repeat the same mistake thereafter,
I'm tired of crying in shame and guilt,
every time I think of my behavior.

Dear Pastor

Dear pastor,
I write to you in deepest humility and curiosity,
I come to you with questions and confessions of a
Worst Sinner,
I remember the sermon you preached the other Sunday,
I couldn't come to your church as my soul has run away,
I hope you understand that I watched you online instead,
and honestly speaking,
it's best for you not to be associated with me in any way.

Dear Pastor,
you said something about God that I did not understand,
to refresh your memory let me quote what you said,
"*God is perfect, and all his children are perfect as well,*"
I heard your church shout mighty,
I think they agreed with those words,
but how can a sinner like me, be perfect in any way?
how can an addict like me, live up to what you said?
or is it not cut-out for me, that no way I can be as perfect?

yours sincerely,
the Worst Sinner.

A Taste of Both Worlds

It was a taste of both worlds,
having my feet dipped into your glory and my sin,
so much into confusion that I thought myself
to be an expert of both darkness and light,
but how can one move shackled on one leg,
and free on the other?
how can I be the *Worst Sinner* today
and be a Christian saint the day after?
how can I think of evil desires
and speak forth the truth?
how can my mind delight in the world
and be sold out to Christ?
let me not be a spit out of your mouth,
for you want your people hot,
and I am lukewarm.

A Stranger Before God

How did I become a stranger to my own God?
how come I do not know what to say
in the presence of my Lord?
did *sin* really take me this far away from Him?
did pride cover my eyes
that I do not recognize my own Father when I pray?
(*forgive me of my sin,*
bridge me back to You with love and grace,
take me back into the family of Saints)

A Crushed Heart

Crush my heart Lord,
break the walls of hatred around it,
remove the pride which seats
on the throne of my decisions,
light my heart on fire,
burn the weeds of anger scattered all over,
wash my heart with your blood,
wipe away the dirt of my sin that so easily entangles,
shine your light on all the dark places of envious thinking,
restore the temple of my heart,
and build a home for your Holy Spirit.

The Worst Sinner: Part 3

His soul was tied not to one, not to two!
the *Worst Sinner* had his soul in cuffs by many women,
like a bounty in the hands of a hunter,
(*or like a carcass in the mouths of the vultures,
this sinner's soul was crushed, not pitied at all!*)
who can mend his broken soul?
who can lose his heart from chains?
who can save this broken vessel?
his hope lies on a *Savior*,
a savior of souls and a conqueror of hearts,
his hope lies on a *God*,
a *God* of love whose throne is mercy.

A Letter to a Friend

Dear friend,
you have changed!
(*don't get me wrong*
it's good that you've changed)
I remember those days when we got wild together,
(*fool around and go to parties together*)
when you could read my mind full of deceptions,
(*and agree to do anything without questions*)
but now you go to church every day,
(*and for that I am super proud of you*)
you have new friends that you run to,
I hear you sing praises on Sundays too,
(*is that why you don't pick up when I call you?*
I text you one minute, you don't reply at all?
only for you to post a bible verse the next minute!)
you see maybe I need help to stop sinning at least a day,
maybe I need your secret to deliver me some way,
or maybe I need a friend to tell me it's possible today,
but I get it old friend,
(*you're wearing white cloths, and I am a blood stain*)
I just hope you say my name as you pray,
you never know maybe your God,
can change my ways one of these days.
    yours sincer*ely,*
    a sinner friend.

Broken promises

It's a personal record for me,
if I counted the times I've come to you
with my tears and promises of
"*I will not do it again*"
because I did it again Lord,
and this time I didn't just make a mistake,
but I made fun of your holy grace.

It is a personal record for me,
if I counted the promises I broke to you
with my prayers of
"*I promise I'll be a better person*"
because I'm not a better person,
at least not on the inside, no way,
and it is on the inside that you want me to change.

A Sinner's Prayer

Heal my body with your stripes,
take away the pain that you paid for
with a crown of thorns,
dig me out of this pit of sins,
stretch your hand towards my dying soul,
let your mercy be the rope that rescues me from abyss,
have your angels escort me to the bosom of my father in faith,
(*don't count me among the wicked,*
don't count my sin as existing)
forgive my rebellion *oh Lord*,
see my lawlessness no more,
write my name on your palms,
let me be a partaker of your *Grace*,
may I not be left out in the book of *Life*,
may I be present at the congregation of the *Saints*.

The Last Time

Did you really mean it?
when you said to me this was the last time?
did you really mean it?
when you made me do the same thing
I constantly repent to God for?
or was it your plan all along?
(*that I dwell in this pool of afflictions,*
that I become a slave to your suggestions,)
did you really mean it?
when you said to me this was the last time?

When a Sinner Judges a Sinner

Our addictions were different,
our sinful lives were quite the opposite too,
(*for he was chained to a substance,*
and I was chained to the images)
yet I thought he was the worst of sinners,
not knowing I was actually the *Worst Sinner*,
I judged him for being different,
(*while we both needed the same forgiveness*)
and I thought I was better,
because my iniquity was hidden better,
I didn't think I was that dirty,
maybe because I appeared clean outside,
but I was wrong you see,
as we all cried to the same deliverer.

A Heart's Prayer

It's me again Lord,
it's me again I come to pray,
with my heart this time,
not with my empty words and praise,
I know you always listen,
to my every word, thought and rage,
but I speak from my heart today,
so a difference I hope to make,
(*please hear me out again,*
for with my heart I come to pray)

Take the Pain Away

Take my pain away,
chase all the hurt in my heart away from me,
cancel all my debt away,
pay my sins with your precious blood you poured for me,
hold me in your arms again,
remind my soul of how much I mean to you.

The Samaritan

Refresh my spirit,
fill the wells of my heart
with the drops of living waters
meant for eternity.

Like the woman on the well,
reveal the wickedness in me,
so that like a book I may be read
in the palms of your hands.

I am the Samaritan,
unworthy of your love,
yet you cared enough
to offer my sinful soul
life that is beyond this life.

The Seed Called Sin

A seed called sin,
germinated into a fruit called death,
first to my soul,
second to my once humble character,
until I met a *God* of resurrection.

The Repenter's Prayer

Dear God,
I come to you with my face down to earth,
not because I am humble,
but because I cannot look up to face you,
my sins have made way to my face,
and my eyes feel shame in your presence,
I met one of your children,
it's funny because he was like me before he came to you,
he said it's possible for me to be like him,
(*he even had the nerve to say that*
my "Worst Sinner" title was already taken
by one of your servants named Paul)
he said that if I too believe in your forgiveness,
I can leave the sinful life and be called your son,
(*and that although my sins are as red as blood*
you have the power to make them as white as snow)
honestly, I didn't look into the bible for verification,
that's because I just believed what he said,
and my belief got me on my knees today,
forgive me God for I have sinned.

yours sincerely,
the Repenter.

Chapter 2

FOUND BY GRACE, EMBRACED BY LOVE

Found by Grace

It was your grace that found me,
my best works couldn't save a hair on my head
against the damnation of the rebels,
how am I better than the others?
I am the *Worst Sinner* every time I see a mirror,
but your love has covered me still,
your word has spoken in my favor,
and your mercy has taken me by surprise,
I want to live my life proclaiming this message,
"*the Worst Sinner has no match, against the grace of God,*
the worst sin is still shallow, against the deep grace of God."

Embraced by Love

Love is the only thing that puts us together,
it is the only thing between a perfect God
and an ever-sinful man like me.

Love is what held a *Messiah* to the cross,
it wasn't the six-inch nails as they made us believe.

Love is what made God give,
it's what made a self-sufficient God run to me
as if I had anything to offer as a favor.

Love is a man, who died for me innocently,
Love is a God, who rose for me victoriously,
Love has a name, *Jesus*.

The Worst Sinner is Saved

In darkness he was caged,
inside the pits there he stayed,
(*without the mark of Christ in him,*
His mind and soul were chained)
but it was You who freed him from hell,
only You were the one who said to him,
"*son, your soul has now been saved.*"

Who am I to be Loved Like This?

I looked into His wondrous eyes,
of a man yet God of ages and eternity,
how graceful it is to be called *His* son,
I could settle for a slave or a mere working being,
but eternal glory for me He planned and arranged,
who am I to be loved like this?
to be loved like I've never ever sinned,
to be cared like I am perfect though flawed by this sin?
who am I to be loved like this?
to be loved like my flaws were imaginary not real,
to be a carrier of glory not the chains of abyss.

I Met Love

I met love,
and it was not a feeling I thought,
I saw love,
and it looked like nothing that can be bought,
I felt love,
and of it the world has never been taught,
I heard love,
and its words alone my heart has forever sought.

Identity Theft

My image was swapped at birth,
(*my eyes couldn't see the face*
of my creator as I walked the earth)
The enemy told me I was a sinner,
(*that I was defeated by my worst behavior*)
but God opened my eyes with the death of Christ,
(*and at His resurrection He confirmed that I belong to God*)

The Grave of the Past

I buried them all in the grave of my past,
all rejection, harassment, in a jar they were glassed,
everything I thought that would last,
is finally buried in what I call my past,
yes, all the bad at first appeared to be vast,
but all his Grace is what I have amassed.

Desiderio Domini

Dear Jesus,
who am I without you?
what am I without you?
(*you love me truly and deeply,
your love for me is even deeper
than the ocean floor*)
what can I compare this love to?
can I compare it to the sand on a beach?
or maybe to the hair on the head of a woman,
all these can be measured in metrics and numbers,
but your love *Lord* is far greater,
greater than the stars of the nights in Middle East,
I crave your love dear *Lord*,
I crave to always be with you,
my tears are looking for you,
(*they want to be finally wiped by you*)
my heart is looking for love that is divine,
the love that can only be given by you,
fill the void in my heart,
let your love fill me through and through,
because I long to be with you,
(*and each coming day is a step closer
to finally be forever with you*)
desiderio domini.

*yours in love,
Elias.*

My Advocate

You clothed my heart with your faithfulness,
you carried my soul in your *Right Hand*,
all this time I thought
that I was the one who came before you,
but it was Christ who stood before me
(*as my advocate*)

First Christmas

On that silent night,
love was held in the hands of a virgin,
the rich, the wise, the simple, the sheep,
saw love crying, all watching in awe,
the heavens rejoiced not silent at all,
for love grew mighty, a *Carpenter*, a *God.*

Son of God

How can I not believe in your Son?
as I looked up the sky for a sign,
like the wise men's star to align,
I wasn't sure that anything divine,
would answer my prayer in time,
but your grace to me is a goldmine,
under the moon light your spirit just shines,
and in my heart your words are confined,
how can I not believe in your Son?
who had all my priorities redefined,
who took my life and had it redesigned?
and gave me a purpose from which I can't run,
how can I not believe in your Son?

The First Faith

I still remember the first days, (*the beginning*)
as our love life took root from the soil up,
I still remember how my little yet strong faith,
produced more than what my mind had imagined,
I remember my fumbling words of prayers,
though entirely out of order but you listened,
to all my words, yawns and interrupting thoughts,
I still remember *Lord* when I marveled at you,
in awe my eyes looking at you,
astonished reading about what I meant to you,
I still remember the first days, (*the beginning*)
as our love life took root from the soil up.

The Story of Jonah and Paul

The story of Jonah and Paul,
both were mighty chosen of God,
both carried messages to hundreds of souls,
both were in a ship bound far from home,
and both faced troubles caused by great storms.

Jonah chose sleep over saving the ship,
Paul chose leadership which saved the ship,
Jonah was desperately running from God,
Paul was faithfully running to God.

but God's grace and mercy saved both their souls,
one to Nineveh and the other to Rome.

Under His Grace

Under the umbrella of your Grace,
I live, I love, and I live again.
under the care of your wings,
I sleep, I wake, and I always pray
under the cover of your salvation,
I praise, I worship, and I always dance
under the twinkle of your smile,
I stand knowing well,
I am forever yours.

The Light in the Dark

In the midst of my darkest hour,
I find your light in me.
All this time my soul
was in fact a torch of your salvation.
I am lit in the dark,
for even though I am in this fallen world,
I am not of it anymore.

Salvation

Salvation belongs to the *Lord*!
as my soul passed through hell
and my body subjected to addictions,
as I was imprisoned in afflictions,
and called by my sin's inclinations,
my future was uncertain,
and my life was purposeless,
your *Right Hand* saw my hopelessness,
and felt the need for my redemption,
I am a product of your grace,
and a son by your adoption,
all my sins are forgiven,
and all my chains are now broken,
salvation belongs to the *Lord*!

When I Doubted Grace

I used to doubt myself a lot,
I never thought my life could have meaning,
I used to question myself a lot,
(*I never thought that only you*
could have the answers I'm seeking)
I took for granted what you spoke to me,
for I thought myself unworthy
of your perfect love for me,
but now I stand corrected,
(*scratch that*!)
now I stand amazed by your patience,
my life is filled with your presence,
and you gave me love, gave me mercy,
and you gave me endless blessings.

CHAPTER 3

BETWEEN VALLEYS AND HILLS

From my Lips to God's Ears

From my lips to God's ears,
are my words of purpose and meaning.

From my lips to God's ears,
are my thoughts mixed with my feelings.

From my lips to God's ears,
sometimes not words but crying and sobbing.

From my lips to God's ears,
like a child I am, so on Him I keep on nagging.

From my lips to God's ears,
I don't need my intellect, but my heart to be pouring.

In-between Places: Part 1

In between prayer and thanksgiving,
is a season of standing and falling
in my warrior faith.

In between crying and testimony,
is a season of knowing and unknowing
the God I claim to confess.

In between supplication and revelation,
is a season of praising and doubting
the very power to create.

In between waiting and getting,
is a season of raising and lowering
the blessing I so expect.

To Call a Father

I call unto the Lord,
with my voice rust
from the cry I had throughout the night.

I call unto my father,
with my face wet
from the tears covering my eyes.

I call unto Him,
who understands my sobbing whispers,
in whom I find the warmth and comfort.

I weep to Jesus,
whose only breath,
can cherish my weary heart.

In-between Places: Part 2

In between Sunday and Sunday,
are my six days of wondering about,
not knowing,
how to stand firm in my faith.

In between Monday and Friday,
are my days stuck in a cage,
not knowing,
how to proclaim salvation.

Thanksgiving

A farmer sold his farm in search of riches,
not knowing that beneath it were acres of diamonds,
a man driven by ambition seeks that which is not fulfilling,
a man ends up empty, lonely for lack of thanksgiving,
dear Lord,
teach my heart to be content but not settling,
to have dreams with eternal motives not perishing,
to be a servant of truth and not a product of lying,
to know that Jesus is everything and I am not lacking,
that His grace is sufficient and nothing is missing,
to value the people I have, not the ones who need impressing,
teach my heart to be content, to be full of thanksgiving.

A Fallen Saint

I fell into the mud, sticky and dirty,
(*can you believe I was a Christian?*)
yet I felt compelled to fall,
over and over and over!
in the pond of fear, shame and regret,
I looked thrice not once!
for a helping hand not judging
my mud-stained dress and heart,
but I was blinded from seeing,
a pond of clean water nearby,
for other *Christians* laughed at me,
surrounding me, making it impossible to see,
my hope for a blameless life.

Rock Bottom

Sometimes we see ourselves going down,
(when we start to drop,
as gravity keeps pulling us down to the ground)
when the people who held us up start to give up,
and they too start to lay us down,
(nothing to hold on to,
no one to catch us not to hit the ground)
we can see the signs of life pointing down,
relationships, friends & family all letting us down,
(but yet we're afraid of calling God,
because we've already let Him down)
Rock bottom. We get up, repeat the circle,
trusting people over God,
Rock bottom. We get up, repeat the same mistakes
that took us down.

Jesus, the Soldier in my War

Fight for me,
be the soldier in my war
(*for I know my battles are your own*)
those who are against me are strong,
(*they have* the power I don't possess,
the money that I can't spend,
and the time *I can't afford to waste*)
the only card in my hand is *you*,
the only bullet I can use is your *name*,
and the only shield I can carry
is my word of *prayer*,
show them who you are to me,
let them see the one I worship,
may they know with all their power
I am still stronger because of you.

Jesus Wept

Jesus wept.
when I exchanged my vision
for a temporary dream,
unfulfilled by ambition.

Jesus wept.
when I looked into heaven,
with dry eyes and resentment,
saying "*it wasn't me who did that sin*".

Jesus wept.
when I continued on living,
not as a man who received,
his healing and grace.

Jesus wept.
when I exploited my gift,
to lie and deceive,
the very people I was called to lead.

For His Sons and Daughters

For His Sons and Daughters,
are baskets of blessings,
but yet to be claimed.

For His Sons and Daughters,
are many signs and wonders,
but yet to be shown.

For His Sons and Daughters,
are the gifts of the Spirit,
but yet to be used.

For His Sons and Daughters,
are the armies of heaven,
but yet to be deployed.

A Cry Instead of Prayer

I cried again last night before the Lord,
For I was asking Him a whole bunch
of angry "*whys*" and "*why-nots*" about my life.

I poured my heart out so hot,
Like a lava melting down from a volcanic mountain
for there was nothing my heart could contain.

I wept my feelings to God,
Because my words were so bitter they could not be said
but somehow I thought my intentions He understands.

Choosing You

Are you mad at me God?
(*okay that's a stupid question*
because your love is always above the roof)
But my heart is dubiously hopping
between your word and my culture,
between your promise and my fear,
My spirit craves your holiness
while my body is into perversions,
Oh! and this free-will that you gave me,
It's freely running into temptations,
(*now let's make a deal*)
Can you just decide things for me?
Do you mind living the remainder
of my life on my behalf?
while I chill and do nothing on my own?
But I get that you're a *gentleman*,
You don't force your way into people's hearts,
For you want me to choose You,
Just as You chose me from the start.

I see you Lord,
not physically, no.
I see you show up
when I hit the break-pads of my life,
I see your work in me as you turn my ironed ego
into a Godlike life-giving humility,
I see you work from above,
(*but it's as if* you are close to me Lord,
closer than *my own breath can be*)
I see your answers,
as I pray to the *One* I cannot see,
hoping to get what I can only call a miracle deed,
I see you Lord,
through my trials and tribulations,
I see you smile over my happiness and excitement,
I even see you when you tell me it's not good for me,
regardless how much I cry to you
in my childlike contention,
I see you Lord.

I Landed on a Star

It feels like landing on a star,
each time, every moment I encounter who you are.

I busk in the bliss and the blessing of your keep,
so my eyes can rest now,
they've had their share of the weep.

It feels like landing on a star,
each time, every moment I encounter who you are.

Piercings on my Heart

I sleep with the stars as my ceiling,
(*as they worship you by shining,*
so I worship you by writing)
I crave for a touch almighty,
one to the heart,
like a dagger piercing through,
not my flesh but my chambers of good and evil.

Thank You, Lord

I thank you, Lord,
for all the good that I have,
for all the extra you provide,
for all the bad which pointed my way back to you,

I thank you for the character shaping temptations,
and the answered prayers which revealed where you are.

I thank you for my blessing and my brokenness,
for my happiness and my bitter tears,
and thank you Lord for being with me,
even in moments I didn't want to be with myself.

In Need of His Hug

Of all the days,
today I need your hug Jesus,
my worries have come up to me,
my anxieties fill up my heart
with unimaginable speedy heartbeats,
nothing seems to be okay in my life,
(*as I take one step forward,*
I also take two steps backwards in this life)
I need to see you in the present with me,
I don't want you to stay a theory that I believe,
I want to be like David oh Lord,
in my own way I want to keep my hope in you my God,
but even if you don't show up as I expect you to,
I still put my faith in you alone.

My New Best Friend

In isolation I found myself,
(*all this time my heart was*
constantly given *to someone else*)
in my world of loneliness, I searched my soul,
(*I never thought* I *could look at myself*
as a stranger from another world)
I shook my own hand as I do a Best Friend,
(*for it took a pandemic for me to realize*
the potential I bring *to my own life*)
I gave my spirit a love that is unimaginable,
(*for in the midst of crowding with people*
I forgot to love myself first before I do someone else)

CHAPTER 4

A FORMER SINNER, A NEW DISCIPLE

A Disciple

I lost my track, no surprise!
and I know you've given me a second chance,
(*a millionth chance is what you actually gave me*)
I take it, I screw it up, I take it again!
the circle of my Christian life is that simple,
I try to be perfect all the time,
(*while I know you told me that I can't be*)
so I end up being a hypocrite instead,
(*doing the things I constantly preach against,*
hurting the very people you love best,
and saying things I don't even demonstrate)
that's not what you want out of me, I know,
so lead me to be who you want me to be,
(*a disciple*)

The Resume

The fact that I was so bad Lord,
was to you the best qualification
that I needed to be your disciple.

The fact that sin resided in me,
was to you the best reason
to forgive me of it all.

The fact that I had no direction,
was to you a necessity,
to gift me with your Holy Spirit.

Easy Christianity

They told me Christianity was easy,
but to lust on a woman is to commit adultery,
and to be angry on a man is to commit a murder.
They told me Christianity was easy,
but I must forgive even those unforgivable,
and I must treat right even those who are wrong.
They told me Christianity was easy,
but I must love even the so-called enemies,
and I must bless all those who curse me.
They told me Christianity was easy,
but my good deeds don't earn me salvation,
and my good works won't make me enter heaven.
They told me Christianity was easy,
but even in my pain I should keep on rejoicing,
and even in my suffering I should keep on hoping.
They told me Christianity was easy,
but to obey God is better than my offering,
and my giving is better than my receiving.
They told me Christianity was easy,
but without faith I cannot get what is mine,
and without faith I cannot even please God.
They told me Christianity was easy,
but the life that I love is no longer my own,
and the plans that I have must be surrendered to Christ.
They told me Christianity was easy,
but for me to live it I need the Holy Spirit,
and for me to grow I need to stay planted in the word.

When the Devil is Hunting a Disciple

Sometimes my past is haunting me,
my previous sins a*nd addictions*
*flash by my eyes r*ight in front of me,
the long-gone regrets and distractions
find their way back into my memories,
I think the devil is frustrated,
so he's trying to make me feel unforgiven,
he seems to forget he's defeated,
as he's trying to have me leave the way of salvation,
in retort I remind him of the cross,
and how gracefully I'm forgiven,
a son of God I'm now called,
the Kingdom of Heaven is my inheritance,
how recklessly I am loved,
and that by Jesus I'm now taken,
he cannot stand the word of God,
so in my words I recite it,
I fill my lips with God's promise
and all the biblical affirmations.

Jealous

I get jealous sometimes!
I get jealous of the people you talk to,
I get jealous of their prayers you answer
I get jealous when they brag of how great you are
and how you've given them endless seasons of laughter
(*I get jealous when they get to call you Dad*
and I get to call you Father)
I get jealous when an unbeliever
gets what I pray for in months and even years after
I get jealous when I pray for a miracle
but face mountains of disasters

Running From God

I ran away from God so fast
as if I was trying to break an Olympics' record,
I took off from Him for the longest time
as if I was a professional marathon runner,
(*But who could've thought?*)
That all my running was actually
leading me back to His heart!
(*who could've thought?*)
In every place I ran to
there He was with His open arms!

I didn't know any better,
just as Paul thought
he was serving God by killing believers,
so was I,
when I did a bad thing with a "*good*" motive.
I was stupid!
when I purposely watered down what was right,
and settled for what was "*good*".
teach my heart to align with your will,
so that I may always be in line with your purpose.

Be in me

(*Dear Jesus*)
Be in me,
live inside my heart,
have my eyes see what you see,
take my feet to where you want me to be,
let my ears listen to the words of life you speak to me,
may my whole body be a vehicle of your promises guaranteed,
(*my heart, my heart!*
pause! take a break,
for Jesus is Lord)
step into the glory of your maker and your protector,
hold firm on to the promise of your savior and lover.

A disciple's hunger

I hunger for more,
I'm not selfish or greedy,
but I just feel I can get to know you better.
I'm not driven by miracles,
not that I don't appreciate
the signs and wonders of a great God,
but to me even the act of breathing
is as profound as the act of walking on water,
this is why I hunger for more.

Dear daughter of God

You were made clean, daughter of God,
your past mistakes were all taken by the Lord,
don't dwell in your past,
quit thinking about the chains of Egypt,
the devil will tell you you're unworthy,
(*that what you did was too heavy to be forgiven*)
but remember a man shed his blood for your life,
(*and who the Son sets free is free in deed*)
so accept that freedom together with its forgiveness,
and at the same time, learn to forgive yourself in the process,
you were made clean daughter of God,
your past mistakes were all taken by the Lord.

A disciple's surrender

I cast them all to you Lord,
all my anxieties and burdens,
I put them on you my God,
all this time I've been a Savior of my own life,
I carried them all in my heart,
I used to trust my own ways,
and I was confident on my own means,
but all through that I was ignorant,
as I put myself on a throne untouched,
I now surrender to you Lord,
on your feet I cast them all,
(*I'm no longer a savior of my soul,*
I'm no longer a driver of my life)

A magnet of grace

Let me be the magnet of your salvation,
Let me attract to you the wicked and the sinners,
Let my life show the possibility of your forgiveness,
Let everything in me become a mirror of your mercy,
Let me be a walking bible to be read in a lifetime,
(*for I may be the only Christ they meet in their struggles*)
Let me be a channel of your love for people,
(*and a proof that God can work through an imperfect person*)
Let me be a living testimony of your greatness,
(*and an existing blessing of the Almighty*)
Let me be the magnet of your grace,
Let me attract to you the lost and the brokenhearted.

As I pray

As I go on my knees
I'm touching heaven,
my face is down to the ground,
but my spirit is up in His presence,
my tears to some are a curse,
but they are beautifying scents for His palace,
for as I go on my knees and pray,
I touch His heart in the heavens.

CHAPTER 5

THE LOST PROVERBS

"Wisdom can be found in submission to God."

—ELIAS KASUNGA

A WISE THOUGHT

Vulnerability is the pathway to trust,
and forgiveness is a medicine for the heart,
what you love is what you attract,
and submission of pride is the beginning of humility,
to believe is to receive, be it spiritually or physically,
the best saint needs grace as much as the *Worst Sinner*,
(*and God is for them both, the lost and the God fearer*)
a good deed is a deposit, a good word is a soft drink,
the mind is a garden, what grows is what you plant,
your behavior is like a dog, either you train it or it runs wild,
your tomorrow is a building, and today is its foundation,
our life on earth is but a practice, real life is in eternity.

Building blocks

Words are like building blocks,
and your life is like a builder's plot,
what you speak shall be built,
what you say shall come to pass,
so train your tongue to be right,
especially when you're hurt.

A Godly journey

To travel alone
is impossible in Christianity,
the enemies and the frenemies
are lined up against your destiny,
don't let your ego speak to you,
(*rather let a brother walk you through*)
don't let your sin pull you down,
(*but tell a sister and have a sit down*)
a hungry lion hunts an isolated prey,
(*and a lone wounded cheetah is worse than a donkey*)
a believer alone is gambling his salvation,
(*but in a company of Saints, a believer is unshaken*)

To pray, to listen

And when you pray,
take time to listen. (*God is speaking to you*)
as you take a moment to read his word,
He speaks again to your heart,
when you meditate in the spirit.
let Him speak, don't rush to get off the knees,
remember your prayer is an invitation,
(*and it's not a one-way street!*)
don't leave him alone while you sleep,
but pull up a chair close to you, just as a friend.
invite His presence in your room,
make an appointment and get excited,
then He'll freely chat with you,
for things in the present, for things of truth.

Time

The One who made it
does not live in it,
for time is a ruler and
a slave of all people.
The lost believe it's so plenty,
yet the wise know of its limit,
how can you tame that which cannot rest?
how can you increase its measure for your own gain?
time is a friend, yet still is an enemy,
for time that is lost has costed so many,
but time redeemed has saved many in eternity.

Born a mistake,
thrown to a river,
and Moses became,
Israel's deliverer.

Born in guilt,
raised as a shepherd,
and David became,
a king and a warrior.

Born in a manger,
raised as a carpenter,
and Jesus became,
the only true savior.

The great confusion

Some things are so risky,
but we want them anyway,
some truths are our healers,
but we deny them someway,
some people are angels,
but we chase them all away,
some prayers have our answers,
but we never say them not a day,
some griefs are cured by laughter,
but we're sad every day,
some solutions are just ideas,
but we bury them on our way,
some things are now a past,
but we keep them on replay,
some things are for the future,
but we want them right away,
some habits are poisonous,
but we have them each on display,
some actions are hideous,
but we show them on screenplay,
you see wisdom has a cost,
and we usually underpay,
and ignorance has a price,
which we constantly overpay.

Divine lessons

Help me learn from your lessons,
help me see the interventions you do in my life,
let me understand your corrections,
for your love has never changed whether I do good or bad,
Help me see that it's better I get swallowed by a whale
(*than sink deep in the belly of an ocean*)
your storms *oh God* are better than the rivers of men,
to walk with you in the valleys of death
is still safer than walking alone on a mountain,
to be poor with you is to be rich,
(*and to have it all without You is extreme poverty*)
Lord hold my soul in your hands for it is yours,
(*for all who hold on to their souls shall never be yours*)

Begin,
think about it,
deep inside your heart and search for it,
find it,
fantasize about it,
make your thoughts around it.

Be crazy about it,
act as if it's the only thing that matters,
do it, fail,
do it again and again!
let the world know it can do nothing
to separate your love for it.

Master it,
Be great at it,
share your passion for it,
and then succeed in it,
by being it.

A man's heart

I am the heart,
not at peace, constantly at war,
full of desires and flaws,
I am the heart,
not at all loving, constantly lusting,
heavy with burdens of hate,
always deceiving the way,
perfectly clothing my rage,
so why do you always say,
"*I follow my heart!*"
don't you know I'm leading you astray?

When you give your life to Christ

When you give your life to Christ,
you don't change from bad to good. Rather,
you are resurrected from death to life.
When you give your life to Christ,
you don't do good to earn salvation. Rather,
you do good because good was done to you.
When you give your life to Christ,
you don't convert to a new religion. Rather,
you are adopted into God's family forever.
When you give your life to Christ,
you don't pretend your way into perfection. Rather,
you are renewed daily into Christ's own image.

What is life if it's not an opportunity?
a humbling moment to be grateful to Him.
What is life if it's not a gift?
a present not asked yet freely given to us.
What is life if it's not a privilege?
a chance to spread His love to the world.
What is life if it's not an honor?
an honor to pursue what God has spoken.
What is life if it's not happiness?
a joy which can only be given by the Lord.
What is life without a calling to answer?
a destiny to fulfil and a race to run.
And what is life without Jesus Christ?
a giver of purpose and the reason to live.

CHAPTER 6

A LETTER TO MY FUTURE WIFE

As I am looking for you

As I am looking for you,
I look to God to find you,
inside His grace to find your heart,
I read His word to get to know you,
for I know you are what He says you are,
I pray to God to make you mine,
for I know His will is better than mine,
I don't follow the world's ways with you,
for you're clearly a citizen of the heavenly realm,
I don't go after your "*obvious*" beauty,
I track your beautiful spirit which is hidden in Christ.

I Love You, Before I Met You: Part 1

I thank God that I love you
even before I met you.
My heart is waiting for you,
and so does my body let me remind you.
I've learnt to cook from my mother,
just in case you need a chef too.
I've started to pray for our daughter,
and our son's prayer is next in line.
I've worked on my anger issues,
you shouldn't worry about that temper of mine.
And don't think I won't be faithful to you,
for I've been faithful even before I met you.

Forgive me

I wasn't genuine all my life,
I lied and lied and lied!
(*to God, myself and to you*)
and even though I haven't met you,
I feel this need to be forgiven by you,
I'm sorry for my previous addictions,
and the sexual escapades not with you,
I gave my body to women,
a body that was meant only for you,
I tell you the truth I regret it,
(*you can ask Christ who had to deal with it*)
I've asked God for forgiveness,
and I've had to forgive myself too,
so now I ask it from you,
I hope you get to forgive me too.

I love you, before I met you: Part 2

I thank God I met Christ before I met you,
(*you see loving Christ is my foundation for loving you*)
and even though I love Christ more than I love you,
the second place is reserved just for you boo,
I can't lie, after Christ I think mostly of you,
I even imagine the excitement of coming home to you,
you see my work is so demanding
but I would gladly spend the day with you,
(*I would call in sick, fake a seizure!*
just to add those hours with you)
my heart is longing for you,
and my body is kept in purity too,
I wish you saw me as I'm writing,
for I'm smiling in the very thought of you.

What more can I ask for?

It was God's love that brought me close to you,
(*and the inner peace you gave my heart,*
the moment I got to know you)
what more can I ask for?
if all of my destiny can be accomplished by you,
what more can I ask for?
if not to settle down and serve my God with you.

Skilled, maybe!

I'm learning new skills can you believe that?
apparently, I'm not an old dog anymore
I can even learn a trick or two,
with few years down the line
I can be a master too,
I'm trying to play a guitar,
so that I sing a song for you,
I can't promise about my voice,
I'm sure you'll learn to love it,
because God loves it too.

Dear *Future Wife*,
I wish I could tell you
that I've planned our lives for us,
but I would be lying to you,
and that's a line I wouldn't cross on you,
I don't have all the answers,
but I know the One with all the answers,
I don't have a sure plan ahead,
but I know the One with a plan for our marriage,
I'm not sure about the riches,
but with Christ we are more than wealthy,
I've gone ahead to commit us to God,
for I know you would want the same too,
our lives are now His,
and His plan is now ours too.

yours in love,
Husband

New Wisdom

So I've become sort of wise you might say,
maybe reading too much of *Proverbs* has that effect,
I've learnt that time can be a friend or an enemy you see,
and I can't commit to something worthy without practice,
I want to be honest with you,
so in my singleness I'm learning about integrity,
I want to be genuine to you,
so in the meantime I've asked Jesus to search me,
I want to always honor you,
so God is humbling me in all my trials and successes,
I never want to mistreat you,
so I've started to do good even to those wishing me harm,
I want to always love you,
so I'm learning from Christ to love unconditionally.

In Your Secret Battles

What should I pray for you today?
you see I came back from work a bit exhausted,
I was going to get my rest in bed,
but I had this burden in me about you instead,
maybe God is telling me something and I need to understand,
I don't know what to pray for,
as yesterday I prayed for your spirit and your health,
but don't you worry my love,
because on my knees I would go for you any day,
the Holy Spirit is the searcher of secrets,
he knows the secret battles you face every day,
with His help I will fight in your battles,
for I am your Knight, and I will protect you against troubles.

CHAPTER 7

AS I WALK INTO ETERNITY

The Son Of God is Coming

Look! He's coming,
up in the clouds He's shining,
the angels around Him are singing,
the Son of God is coming.

Look! He's coming,
and up in the clouds we're going,
the children of God rejoicing,
the joy in us' overwhelming.

Look! He's coming,
the King of kings is coming,
but currently He's still knocking,
in your heart He's calling.

As I enter the Gates

I cannot wait to enter the gates,
in the city I was promised I cannot wait,
to be in a place free from all the hate,
and to finally be lifted off these weights.

I cannot wait to enter the gates,
to see my *Savior* who took my mistakes,
to sit on his lap and share in his plate,
I'm looking forward to meet him at the gates.

The Feast of the Lamb

At the feast of the lamb we'll gather,
and with Him we'll cherish forever,
we'll be perfect at last with our *Maker*,
with all the saints and the angels together,
there's no sin, not even as small as a feather,
no evil, no sorrow and definitely no anger,
not a soul will be sad, and no one will feel hunger,
we'll all know each other, for we're brothers and sisters,
and our God will be there, our loving heavenly father.

Don't cry for your loved ones in Christ,
(*don't be sad for the passing of the saints*)
remember this world was never their home,
and Jesus said they're only just sleeping,
look forward to that reunion,
for the joy we'll have is beyond comparison,
be keen to see them again,
for they'll all be with us at the final resurrection,
(*don't you know we'll be together forever?*
don't you know heaven is for eternity?)
so rejoice for their lives though brief in time,
as it's better to be absent from this body,
only then we'll be present with God,
so don't cry for your loved ones in Christ,
(*don't be sad for the passing of the saints*)

Jesus, My All in All

Jesus is my all in all,
at his throne are my pleasures forever more.

Jesus is my eternity wrapped up in a person,
his presence is a heaven my heart longs for.

To the One Who Led Me to Christ

Thank you for accepting the calling,
(*the call in your heart to lead me to Christ*)
I was lost and I was dead in the spirit,
all that I did was destroying my life,
you gave me a gift of which I cannot pay,
you gave me Christ and my life was changed,
thank you for accepting the calling,
(*the call in your heart to lead me to Christ*)

ACKNOWLEDGEMENTS

1. To my Lord and Savior Jesus Christ, who is the giver of talents and gifts. It is an honor to serve Him with my writing.
2. To my parents who never knew I was a writer in the first place. I hope with this work they get to see the other part of their son.
3. To all my friends who never gave up on me. Thecla, my cheer leader, Baina and Novatus who basically pushed me to be serious with writing, to Sarah who always reminded me that the first copy of this book belongs to her, and to countless others who stood by me.
4. To my first readers (Pastors Pamela Austin & Ephy Musiba, Dorothy Kilewo and Nancy Lazaro) who gave me hope after reading the first drafts and most importantly corrected my grammar mistakes.

ABOUT THE AUTHOR

Elias Kasunga is a poet and a writer whose prayers, psalms, poems and quotes have been shared primarily in his home church, among friends and his Instagram page. He is a lawyer by profession and currently lives and works in the city of Dar es Salaam, Tanzania, East Africa. He enjoys reading anything from books to articles to even tweets while at the same time writing his thoughts everywhere and anywhere.

He is a member and a servant of the Ocean International Community Church, Dar es Salaam, Tanzania where he leads a small weekly connect group and serves in other multiple church ministries.

You can reach out to him through the following ways:

Personal email: ellykasunga@gmail.com

Instagram page: @elias_kasunga

www.ingramcontent.com/pod-product-compliance
Lightning Source LLC
LaVergne TN
LVHW020639100826
845148LV00012B/2243